Confessions Of A Muse

Poems

Faye Pantazopoulos

BookLeaf
Publishing
India | USA | UK

Made with ❤ on the BookLeaf Publishing Platform
www.bookleafpub.in
www.bookleafpub.com

Dedication

Dedicated to my my father, and my two godmothers

Preface

Acknowledgements

1. Where the Stars Fall

I met you
where the stars fall.
In the city,
in a rough neighborhood.
It was dark and your eyes
lit the sky with green.
Those northern lights
sparkling as you smiled.
You brushed my hand
and we sipped
pink wine
and shared stories
while the moon watched
knowing and smiling.
She knew when we parted
it would be the beginning
of forever.
In the rough neighborhood
on the second floor
where ghosts still floated

across hardwood floors
and the wine flowed
as Kate's songs filled
the empty rooms
a forever kind of love
blossomed.
Your gold heart
made the impossible
possible.
And I fell
like a star
ever after
into your
night sky.

2. Hunting Season

It's hunting season.
Arrows sharpened deadly
hang over her shoulder,
all the way down her back.
They're tracking deer.
She has other prey in sight.
She doesn't sleep.
She is back in those woods
running only to be surrounded .
No one heard her scream.
The knife left a scar on her arm.
She wears it like a badge
to remind herself to
never be prey again.
Tonight she hunts.
Her arrows quicker
than guns.
She sets her eyes on
the prey.

3. Huntress

The huntress sleeps.
Souvenirs of the kill
decorate her body.
She sleeps lightly
these days.
Listens and watches.
The scent of her prey
is wafting on the night wind.
Musky with a trace of sage.
She sits up.
This is the night
she makes the kill.

4. Persephone

This is how it happened.
She wasn't taken.
She fell.
Tripped on a tree root into
the darkness
only to realize it was
a pair of eyes
dark as the entrance
to hades.
Lips full and parting
smooth talker
filled her head with fantasy
wove the wreath of lilies
crowning her head
burned his name into
her skin til it bled
and watched as his blood
seeped into her heart.
Only them did he smile
as he pulled out the knife

to cut it out.
These drops of blood
she follows their trail
to find her way back
to light, to herself,
to who she was before
she sold a fantasy
to a boy who cost her
her soul.

5. Desert

I can feel the emptiness most
here in the desert.
Though the sky is
painted in warm colors
and the heat burns
I feel cold.
You burned out fast.
I have come through
the ache of silence
to understand
and to blaze with fire.
You forget there's
a lion inside this mouse.
In the stillness
I put the pieces together,
and sometimes I still cry.
But there's only so much
water can do.
It's fire's turn to make a move.
I wait in the desert .

I have all that i need
to rise.

6. Sycamore Trees

Tall and white and ghostly,
they greet me at every turn
limbs out and open.
I'm not afraid.
I hear they grant
protection, clarity.
Maybe they will
clear away the clouds
and the rain
from my eyes.
Maybe they will
protect my heart.
These sacred trees
that stand in my path
at every bend in the road
they greet me.
I build a nest here
in the crook of their arms,
lay my head down
and dream.

7. Leo

In the month of the lion,
in the land of sun
I awake.
I realize I was foolish.
For months now
I peeled away the layers,
one after the other.
It took weeks to get at
the truth.
To see myself as you
must see me.
I turn around.
The night is a black cape
slung over my shoulder.
I whisper goodbye
And step into the light.

8. Witch's Cove

I know the way
to witch's cove,
the winding leafy roads.
I hang a left at the edge
of the crescent moon.
Follow the harbor lights
flickering over the still water.
It's a stone's throw
from your cave.
Twelve steps you could
take and I'd be in your arms.
I could use a little black magic
but I'd rather test fate.
I keep diving deeper and
deeper off the crescent edge
into the sound
Where the shore
curves into a moon.

9. Crashing Waves

We crashed like waves
off the island sound.
I'd watch you ride
And break and dive
Always rising.

I was the moon and
you were the tide.
Tied together.
The pull too strong.

But those demons of yours
always got in the way.
They were in every bottle
hiding behind every word
You didn't say.

And when I left it was a
sunny summer day.
I was riding the waves

and you were shut away.

You can always reach me, you know,
Was the last thing you said.
And every time you're in the dark
battling those demons,
I dream you're calling
my name.

And I send you my love
no matter who
my heart belongs to these days.
You still can't separate the
moon from the tide.

10. Persephone in Spring

Persephone emerges
from the gates of Averno.
It's spring
the light she brings
spreads.
She no longer remembers
her true name.
She carries his darkness inside her.
He - captor, lover, husband, god.
Nature rejoices at her freedom,
her return from darkness.
But the red fruit binds her to the underworld.
Here the light erases the nights
held captive in darkness.
Erases the chains and the savage way
the god claimed her.
She remembers being
young and pure the day
the darkness swooped in.
The god abducting her

eternal nights captive in his lair
stripped of her innocence
her name changed.
He made her queen.
Her reward for being
his possession.
She looks at her reflection
in the still lake.
No longer a girl
a woman stares back
with haunting dark eyes -
still beautiful but not innocent.
His touch has filled her
with knowledge,
changed her,
left traces of darkness
where there was only light.
And she craves him now
Captor, lover, husband, god.
Come to miss the dark
as much as she once
missed the light.
She, queen of the underworld
stands at the gates
of her kingdom
understanding now

there is no light
without his darkness.

11. Eve

The truth is
she didn't reach
for the apple.
It fell in her hand
so red and ripe
and sweet.
She couldn't resist
a bite.
She didn't see
the serpent
until it was too late.
The truth is
the fall into
darkness
was better
than the light
in the garden.

12. Notre Dame

I stood alone out on her steps
staring up at the windows
medallions of cut colored glass.
The gargoyles watched me
followed me inside then back out
to the crepe cafe, inside my head
where I held a conversation
with my father on the other side.
Now I watch her burn
along with my memories.
Before there were iPhones,
before Instagram,
before I was afraid to be alone
She stood with me.
But even as the flames consume her,
she shines a sign of eternal hope.
She may be down but she will
rise again as will I. She assured me.
We are made of fire she whispers.
Phoenix.

13. Fairy Godmothers Do Exist

Fairy godmothers do exist
I have proof.
After all, I was blessed with two.
From Stella, mother says I got my
sense of style.
A love of fur and jewels and anything that
sparkles.
You know, I always could accessorize.
From Maria I got my edge -
a passion for whiskey, rock n' roll
and a streak of independence hard to curb.
But the proof of their fairy godmother status
is depicted throughout my childhood.
There's photos of my magical merry-go-round birthday
cake,
dresses and baubles and a penchant
for rescuing me from myself.
There in the photos Stella always glowing
a halo of light surrounding her.

And light is what they named me.
Light, daughter of the sun, goddaughter to the star.
Stella, you're a star now
and my light dims without you here.
I will wear every sparkly bauble
to catch your reflection and keep you close.

14. January and June

She roars in, Miss January
heralding a new decade.
Dressed in feathers and pearls
she throws up her hands and
tosses a shiny full moon to the wolf
who misses the catch blinded, he says,
by falling stars.
Make your wishes now,
January whispers and I'll have
June deliver them.
She's a tiny red crab
curled up in the safety of the moon.
She and January share secrets
over coffee somewhere by the sea.
Now June is preoccupied.
Her shell is soft and she fears exposure.
January is hard and sharp and cold like diamonds.
She offers June her icy hands and says here,
let me touch your heart it's burning up again.
And with that June knows she's strong enough

to survive whatever the rat and the wolf
and the roaring twenties have in store.

15. You Were Wild

You were wild
where are you now?

I can see you now
with your tired tattoo
slinging an axe
like it meant harm to you.

Wearing my lingerie
and sipping your juice
telling me baby
I'm breaking the rules.

I knew what I said
would get back to you.
The demons you paint
live inside of you.

Orange elephants
against purple skies

and you never knew
you were colorblind.

You loved me, you said
but I'd never do.
But you're still alone
love isn't for you.

You were wild.
Where are you now?

16. August

I'm a sucker for a man
with a sexy walk,
a slow swagger.
You know the kind.
Clint Eastwood stride
like nobody's watching
but still putting on a show.
That's how August strolled in.
Late but still a surprise
burning up the sky.
The sunflowers wilt
under his gaze.
He is hot sun and honey bees.
He stirs up storms
raises up the corn and
paints the sky with flames.
Yawning as he lays down
like a lion stalking his prey.
"Bring me a bourbon,"
I think I hear him say

Only later, do I realize he said
"Virgin"
After midnight
when, like every ruler,
he requires
sacrifices.

17. October

October blankets the lawn
in a confetti of leaves -
yellow and red and orange.
I spend a few extra minutes
under the down comforter
contemplating the changing light
and how it filters through
the yellow and gray curtains.
You have my coffee waiting
when I stumble into the kitchen.
I cradle it and let it warm
my hands as we say good morning.
Inside I'm falling back into
a waking dream that haunts me.
A dream of lives lived before
and all the secrets they have
left buried inside me.
I smile at something funny
I'm sure you just said.
I'm safe here, under the starry blanket

Cats at me feet, you by my side.
The coffee has gone cold in my hands
as the dream fades.

18. Before Times

We've been in jail for about a year.
Nowhere to run.
Nowhere to hide.
Captives in our own homes.
Chained to sofas, laptops, cellphones.
We live online, onscreen - virtually.
We reminisce about the "before times".
Hugging hello and goodbye.
Eating and drinking at parties.
Traveling - especially traveling. Freely.
Stopping at new places along the way and meeting
strangers bare faced.
I try to remember when was the last time I traveled
without a mask.
DC last March.
Before the lockdown.
But still nervous.
The city was eerily quiet.
Hours in the National Gallery.
Turmeric lattes in a coffee shop.

Dinner at an Indian restaurant sitting at the bar.
Ubering back to our hotel for scotch in the hotel lobby.
The cherry blossoms just beginning to bloom on the day
we left.
Their bubblegum pink shades of innocent joy spreading
across blue skies and brick buildings.
Returning home to one last outing in my new green
dress.
Wine tasting at shelter harbor with a writer friend bare
faced
but the shadow of the virus looming over us.
I dreamt last night of Ancient Greek temples. Maybe
Delphi.
We were recreating them. Like the backdrop in my
wedding photo.
And I wondered why.
Maybe because we're afraid we'll never see them again -
the ancient ruins,
the Egyptian pyramids, the Eiffel Tower.
For five hundred dollars we can fly to Hawaii I tell
husband.
Round trip. Nonstop. Out of Boston.
Book it he says.
But I hesitate.
What will people think? We're not supposed to travel.
We're still in prison I tell him.
Maybe we can wait til June for that trip to Napa.

A boring conference already paid for a year ago.
Canceled then postponed and now tentatively
rescheduled.
For a whole year I've been anticipating seeing the
redwood forest.
To feel something again.
To feel both small and insignificant
and yet part of the world again.

19. Writing

Words spill
and leave stains
you can't remove
like coffee
or blood.
Permanent.
They echo
even after
you turn the page.

20. The Sculpture Garden

I went back
to pick up the pieces
shattered on the garden grounds.
Slices of my heart
in triangular shards
like the Picassos hanging
on the walls inside.
Muddy from my tears
waterlilies run green to blue
to violet
violent like your words
that cut like those
chickenwire sculptures
that made my hands bleed.
I don't remember leaving,
how I made it on the train,
how I got home.
I remained a Pollock tangled mass
of lies for decades -
a victim and the offender -

all at once.
Who could blame you?
It took me 30 years
to forgive that girl and
her Gatsby tongue.
The sculpture garden
is soaked in rain
the broken chain
still there.
I stare at it from above
out the window
silent.

21. Sizzle Reel

She carries the moon
to me
tucked between her wings
but it's still
just out of reach.
I open my hand
and catch only
stardust,
fine and silvery.
It evaporate
like dreams.
Were we really there?
It's all so fragmented.
Words, places, touch and taste.
Is this what it looks like
when your life
flashes before your eyes?
A sizzle reel
a falling star
a moon just out of reach

tucked between
a pair of wings.